A Taste of 'Funny'

A Taste of 'Funny'

For the 'Rhyme' of your Life

Doris Faran

First published in 2005 by:
Doris Farran

© Copyright 2005
Doris Farran

The right of Doris Farran to be identified as the author of this work has been asserted by her in accordance with the Copyright, Designs and Patents Act 1988.

All Rights Reserved
No reproduction, copy or transmission of this publication may be made without written permission. No paragraph of this publication may be reproduced, copied or transmitted save with the written permission or in accordance with the provisions of the Copyright Act 1956 (as amended).

ISBN: 0 9534925 4 0

Printed and bound in Great Britain by:
ProPrint, Riverside Cottages, Old Great North Road, Stibbington, Cambridgeshire PE8 6LR

Other Books by the Author:

'Pictures From A Life'
'Ain't It A Game Eh!'

An 'Autobiography of Nobody in Particular'

Tranquil Thoughts
'Pleasing Poems'

An Unfinished Symphony –
A True Life Love Story

Some 'Opes of Brody Street, E.1.
A Moving Yet Most Humorous Story
of an East End Family, Set Before and During
The Terrible Blitz of World War II.

INTRODUCTION

Doris Farran continues to draw upon many variations in her long eventful life.

Even at the age of eighty five years, she still feels stimulated enough to put into words, some sober, some quite humorous, waggish events, which will amuse and titillate the reader in this new selection of poems, a sequel to:

Tranquil Thoughts
'Pleasing Poems'

*"Look around with eyes open wide,
Do not give but a fleeting glance.
The best things in life are free, they say,
Take heed or you may miss the chance."*

DEDICATION

My thanks to all my family and friends for providing me with the means of sharing many of their colourful experiences both comical and dramatic.

CONTENTS

Inspiration	1
The Vagabond	2
Wishful Thinking	3
Knees Up	4
It's all Outside my Window	5
Meals on Wheels	6
Deliverance	7
When we Grow Up	8
Potpourri	9
Those were the Days My Friend	10
Annie	12
The Rustle of Winter	14
The Blackbird	15
Booty Full	16
Balloons that Pass in the Night	17
The Good Old Days	19
Neighbours	22
A Visit to the Hospital	23
Simply the Best	24
My Old Gamp	25
It all Went Up the Spout	26
Drakes Glum!?	28
Unfinished Symphony	29
Boo Hoo!	30
Isolation – I am Deaf!	31
Dusk	32
Up the Pole – A Tall Story!	33
Junk Mail	35
Mum's the Word	36
Just Doodling!	37
My Venice	38
Jobs	39
Images	40
Misty Memories	41
Did it Really Happen?	42
Twas one of those Days	43
A Pair of Pants	44
The Cruise	45
Harvest Time	47

Our Street	48
How's Zat!	49
Misgivings	50
Kids Stuff	51
Hail! Glorious Spring	53
An Ode to Mothers Day	54
Guy Fawkes Night	55
Christmas Presence	56
Hatched, Matched and Despatched	58
Those Days When	60
Dunkirk's Little Ships – Remember?	61
What's a Doodlebug – Mum?	62
Blood Red Poppies at the Cenotaph	63
Nothing is Forever	64
Get Cracking!	65
My Home	66
New Horizons	67
David	68
A Letter to my Son	69
Barbie Girl	70
A Letter to my Daughter	71

INSPIRATION

Give me some space, a book, a pen,
As under a tree in a shady glen,
I'll lay and ponder wondering how,
To describe the feelings I have right now.

As on my bed of moss I lie,
And watch the clouds fleet o'er the sky,
I'll feel at peace with the world I know,
Praying it could be for all, - but No!

For there are those of a different creed,
Who thrive on hatred, lust and greed,
Could it be, that perhaps one day,
Each soul could find a better way.

To feel the peace that I have found,
Here as I lie, on mossy mound,
There is so much more in life than hate,
Goodwill and contentment only love can create.

THE VAGABOND

Ghostly wraiths glide silent, thru' the mist,
Figures of creatures long since dead.
Eerily searching, touching me cold,
Amid silence where shadows, follow my tread.
Along cavernous passages blackened and dim.
Where river laps lifeless against the quay.
A doleful moon hangs heavy in cloudless sky,
Giving no solace to a vagrant like me.

I shiver and pull my kerchief up tight,
And scurry back, from whence I come.
As downstream, a horn blasts thru' the fog.
'Tis no place for a homeless bum.
Black and sinister, a shape looms nigh,
A cargo ship heads out to sea,
Cold as stone, I capitulate,
For this is no place for a fool like me!

WISHFUL THINKING

If only I were a Red Balloon,
I'd disappear from sight.
To where there is no sound to rend,
My maiden voyage flight.

Weary of my earthly lot,
Of buses that run late.
Rising early every morn,
Just two of the things I hate.

Annoying idiots on the train,
The din from a rave next door.
A car that delights in breaking down,
Visits from Mother-in-law.

P.C. software, floppy discs,
Mobile phones and such
Hi-fi, DVD, surfing the net!
To me, they don't mean much.

I'd hover and glide so gracefully,
Where no fume, pollutes the air.
Discovering peace and solitude,
On my journey, to who knows where!

I'll find my real Utopia,
Maybe sight it very soon.
As I loop and glide, cruise and soar,
I am that Red Balloon!

KNEES UP!

Come let's go for a cycle ride,
It's lovely to feel the breeze.
Tearing away through the countryside,
Showing all your knees.

Isn't it great, out in the fresh air,
I'll beat you up that hill.
Over the top, then down again,
Lumme, ain't it a thrill?

Through pastures new and meadows green,
Pausing to rest at stiles.
I never knew it could be such fun,
Peddling for miles and miles.

Stopping a while on hillocks high,
Full of wonder at the sight.
Of rolling plains mid fields of gold,
Fills one with sheer delight.

Now you can keep your smoky old towns,
Stuffy buses and the like.
Trains that never run on time,
I prefer to ride me bike!

IT'S ALL OUTSIDE MY WINDOW

I sit and watch, by window wide,
And see the world go by outside.
People on their way to town,
People white and people brown.

I've learned to know them all by sight,
Some uncivil – some polite.
Some they smile – some they don't
Others will – others won't.

A woman with her little dog,
Out for his early morning jog.
With a joyful bark, a yelp of glee,
He makes a bolt, for the nearest tree.

A bunch of schoolboys having a scrap,
Disturbs the dog, who starts to yap.
Out from a yard emerges a cat,
Dog takes one look, and that is that!

The cat, he's smart, he's off like a light,
He's not hankering after no fight.
A chappie, driving a battered van,
'Any iron' – he shouts – 'Old pots and pans' –

A bloke on a bike, he tears past,
As if next minute, will be his last!
A couple of women stand tittle-tattling,
With the milkman, his bottles rattling.

Who's this fellow so glum and surly,
It's the postman, for once he's early!!
Down the street, here comes a copper,
Clutching his truncheon – Boy! What a whopper.

There's the paperboy, and he's late,
I wish he'd shut the bloomin' gate.
I've sat here ages, on me backside!
'Where's me flippin' Dial A Ride?'

MEALS ON WHEELS

Watch out Matey, - here they come,
All nicely cooked and neatly done.
Mind that lamppost, - whoops! Too late!
There goes me chops and veg off plate.

Now lets see, its where to next?
Its old Ma Carey's or she'll be vexed.
"Sorry can't stop, I have to dash,"
"With her helping of Sausage and Mash."

Down the hills at maximum speed,
Here come the dinners ready to feed
those eager souls at their garden gate,
Forks at the ready, they stand and wait.

Sal Jones, she's partial to our Plum Pud,
She swears it does her bunions good.
Put in her slippers as an extra sock,
Or as a wedge when the door won't lock.

What would they do without us lot,
And cannot get their Lamb Hot Pot?
Hurrah! for the chance of good square meals,
So hats off to – 'Our Meals on Wheels!'

DELIVERANCE

When you believe the world has stopped
for you, just look around.
So many straws to grasp out there,
Salvation to be found.

I know I've been there, I lost hope,
So pick yourself up, and start again.
As countless rewards are waiting there,
No endeavour – then no gain.

I searched with faith, for peace of mind,
And took what fate could bring.
For already there before your eyes.
In truth, you'll find, just everything.

The sunshine of a Baby's smile,
Stars that tumble from a velvet sky.
Cotton wool clouds, in heavens of blue,
There's wealth out there, for you and I.

Scents of roses, freshly plucked,
Newly mown grass, after the rain.
Sounds of music, of birds' sweet song,
As you walk along a leafy lane.

Long, long ago, I had a dream,
Contentment I would find.
My dream came true, surmounting all,
I regained my peace of mind.

WHEN WE GROW UP

What lies ahead, - for us all!
Would we be short, would we be tall.
Years they passed, and so we found,
Life's all part of a merry-go-round.
We sighed, we cried.
We moaned, we groaned.
We skipped, we quipped.
We giggled, we wriggled.
We screamed, we dreamed.
We moped, we hoped.
We yawned, we mourned.
We played, we prayed.
We hummed, we drummed.
We clapped, we scrapped.
We gaped, we scraped.
We dressed, we blessed.
We gushed, we blushed.
We versed, we cursed.
We betted, we jetted.
We teased, we pleased.
We panted, we ranted.
We worked, we shirked.
We glowed, we rowed.
We bossed, we crossed.
We rallied, we dallied.
We tarried, we married.
We boasted, we toasted.
The life that lay ahead.

POT-POURRI

Nosegays of blossom on creamy wall,
When from my bed I deign to peep.
First to welcome me at dawn,
As I awake from drowsy sleep.

My little bower is bathed in light,
Rays of gold, cross o'er my bed.
Throwing from me the cloak of night,
As with joy I stir, to raise my head.

Once more, my room has come to life,
Dusky pink blooms, caress the eye.
Embraced am I, by their heavenly scent,
While here in my arbour, I choose to lie.

Arise! Arise! They seem to say,
Life's an ever-flowing stream.
Time is much too precious, so,
Don't just lay there, and dream!

THOSE WERE THE DAYS MY FRIEND

Here deep in thought,
Though little to report.
I'll write this ditty,
Now isn't it a pity?
Since you and I,
Tho' only just chicks,
We got up to tricks,
Out there in the park,
Till way after dark.

And out in the Sun,
Didn't we have fun?
The things that we did,
When just a kid.
Life was all honey,
Full, rich and funny.
Can't remember it all,
I was short, you were tall.
Like Revnell and West,
Do you remember their jests?

And then we were twenty,
Of joys there were plenty.
You were a daisy,
I was bone lazy.
Your hair was frizzy,
I was just dizzy.
Remember the hops?
They were the tops.
How short our skirts,
They labelled us flirts.

Had lots of Beaus,
Bid many Adios.
I was thin you outsize,
A bit older, but more wise.

I knew nothing at all,
But nice to recall.
The days, they were long,
Yet sadly all gone.
As if in thin air!
Can anyone tell me Where?

ANNIE

Short and fat, she wears no hat,
She can't get one to fit her,
Her mass of hair, makes everyone stare,
Who's that? Did someone titter?

She puts Harpo Marx to shame,
Standing there like a sore thumb,
When in a crowd they laugh out loud,
Poor Annie – does she look glum!

She hangs her head, and wipes her eye,
And pleads with them to stop,
'Don't worry love,' they hasten to add,
'You'd make a bloomin' fine mop!'

Poor Annie now, she's met a man,
He seems a nice enough fella,
They never worry when it rains,
She makes a damned good umbrella!

A lively thrush, seizing his chance,
Laid a batch of eggs in her hair,
"Oh dear!" She said, "This is the end!"
And cried out loud, "S' not fair!"

Yet not to worry, Sympathisers all,
Or sigh for poor Annie's plight,
A farmer's now got a new thatch on his roof,
It is a magnificent sight!

Ann's crowning glory is up with the birds
She has no need to grouse.
Tho' Annie's got her head in the clouds,
The rest of her's in the house!

But shed no tears for Annie now,
She's finally made her mark,
Her eyes they gleam like beacons there,
On the Farmhouse roof in the dark.

So the moral of this tale is this,
And we can honestly say,
Mock not poor Ann, we're equal see,
We *all* have a part to play.

THE RUSTLE OF WINTER

Green Willow, fronds swaying, fanning the ground
neath my feet, as I look around, for petulant Pansy
that once bloomed fair, amid nosegays of blossom
in my garden where, now oceans of hue and Summer
gives way to the dolour and sadness of an Autumn day.

On Evergreen and Fir, hoar frosts rest, sparkling
on silken webs of the spiders test
and toil, as from frowning Oak, leaves flutter down,
see-sawing to bed on cushions gold and brown.

The purple curtain of Winter will soon unfold,
to snows of diamond white, as Nature boldly
gathers all to sleep, in the deep still of the night.
Should you – storm or gale, - show your might
with bitter winds you gust and rend,
as at my trees you strain to bend, so tarry not,
you can bring no frown, - for you will never,
ever bring them down.

'Twill be, 'ere long after sad winter's hush,
my trees will once again wake,
to the sweetest sounds of the Thrush

THE BLACKBIRD

What is it about Spring on a balmy Eve,
That can put back a smile on a doleful face,
When it touches a timid ear in a noisy world.
Tis the Blackbird!

As he warbles away on treetops high,
Softening the darkening world with his song.
As all nature prepares to shut up shop,
We are fully aware t'will be 'ere long.
We'll hear the Blackbird!

Who will wake you once more at break of dawn,
And again his message will be trilling out
A new day has begun and all is well,
So what is it we can ne'er do without?
Tis the Blackbird!

Alas one day he will fly away,
To pastures new and leave behind,
The sweetest memory of his song,
Which now he sings in climes more kind.
Who? Tis the Blackbird!

BOOTY FULL

Not only cobwebs in Grandma's loft,
Where on a rainy day t'was oft.
I'd climb up thru' the old trap door,
There a hoard of treasure, to explore

A wooden chest, is first I see,
Lock stiff and rusty, 'where's the key?'
As a child in here, I loved to hide,
Curled up small, when once inside.

When new, a valued useful trunk,
Filled now only, with useless junk.
This moth-eaten shawl belonged to Gran.
With her opera glasses, black lace fan.

Great Grandma's mitts, high button boots,
Grandad's rusty, musty suits.
Umbrella stand, which stood in our hall,
With an old cracked mirror, no use at all.

A baby's cot, needed no more,
Children's games, and toys galore.
Sewing machine, an old tin bath,
Tarnished brass fender, from the hearth.

There a calor gas stove, electric fan,
All these and more belong to Gran.
Why does she keep things, on this scale?
They'd fetch a bomb, in a car boot sale!

BALLOONS THAT PASS IN THE NIGHT

Dry your eyes now, don't cry child,
You knew it would happen one day.
Nothing lasts forever you know,
Here today, gone tomorrow, they say.

Your lovely balloons, where are they now?
Maybe gone to a better place.
But you'll never really lose them you know,
So put back that smile upon your face.

Imagine them as you knew them once,
Joyfully playing up high,
Caught on top of that telegraph pole,
Silhouetted against the sky.

Remember the cheer they gave to you,
Every time you happened to glance.
Up where no wind or deluge of rain,
Could disturb their merry dance.

Just remember how they used to be,
When they were in their prime.
Your very own cheeky happy balloons,
Having a wonderful time.

Then sad to say, nobody cared
Anymore to look up and say.
How the blazes did they get there?
They'd shrug and go on their way.

Then one bright and sunny morn,
Just like another day.
But this one was different, I'll tell you why,
For we saw to our dismay.

This man, definitely up the pole,
An idiot, stupid or canned?
It could have been his lot, the silly clot,
Cos' he had this knife in his hand?

The unfeeling bloke, with one mighty stroke,
He cut the balloons asunder.
We were appalled and what he was called,
Did he hear us we hoped, we wonder?

For now they're no more, just a memory to store,
But miracles can happen they say.
You'll pull back your blind, one morning to find,
More beautiful balloons at play.

There must be reasons, for this child,
Are we going round the bend?
We'd better pull our socks up soon,
Or us to the shrink, they'll send!

But we don't care now, do we love?
Gotta do something to pass the time.
Now I must be quick, 'cos it's done the trick,
And now way past me bedtime.

Goodnight!!

THE GOOD OLD DAYS

I'm no chicken and it's no joke,
Yet far from over the hill.
Tho' my knees may creak, I wobble a bit,
There's lots of time to kill.

I own a wealth of memories,
Have seen a lot of change.
In the many years I've lived through,
To some, would now seem strange.

Growing up was a challenge when,
It was not all milk and honey.
Mum pawned clothes, and things for food,
Becos' we had no money.

Most days newspaper, was our cloth,
On the table, when we fed.
If we didn't do as we were told,
It was, 'Right you, - up to bed!'

Dad stood knocking back the pints,
At the bar of his local pub.
As Mum stood sweating at the sink,
Giving his shirts a scrub.

The wash went through the mangle,
That stood out in the yard.
Tho' drying clothes in winter,
Was always ruddy hard!

Hours we'd spend out in the street,
Running, jumping, skipping.
Then Mum would call, 'come, get your tea,
But there's only bread and dripping!'

Learning the ten times table,
Grappling with sums and spelling.
But it was great, - playing outside,
Kids screaming, and kids yelling.

And scrumping in the orchards near,
For apples from the tree.
Stuffing them up, under our vests,
'Hope the farmer, didn't see!'

Come Saturday morn, - A picture show,
To see Roy Rogers and Trigger.
Spending a ha'penny on chewing gum,
We'd stretch it to make it bigger!

In Spring then, were hot cross buns,
Summer, the ice cream van.
Come Autumn, it was chestnut time,
Winter, the Muffin Man.

Christmas – nice, if we had some toys,
When shops were pretty, lights so bright.
Pressing noses on to window panes,
We'd look – we'd hope – we might!

There was no telly, in them days,
Radio – just a dream.
Music Hall, a Xmas treat,
Chaplin was a scream.

Mum would take us for a walk,
Trundling behind the pram.
Hungry, tired, our feet would ache,
Why couldn't we go by tram?

Then us kids, we'd have a scrap,
Mum would go near barmy.
Saying – 'I wish you'd all grow up,
And go and Join the Army!'
(But she really didn't mean it!)

Forever she, weighed down with care,
Would wonder – how to cope.
Though life it wasn't much fun those days,
You always lived on hope.

Hoping it would improve one day,
And be no more provoking,
But saying that now, as we look around,
Cor' Blimey! – You must be joking!

NEIGHBOURS

There are neighbours, who are very nice,
And neighbours you could throttle!
Those who keep you awake at night,
When, they've been at the bottle.

It is better for you at party times,
When you're worried about the racket.
As it's always wise to invite them too,
Then they cannot demand – now pack it!

And when their cat rakes up your bulbs,
Their dog desecrates your lawn.
It you make a fuss, they retaliate,
Then you wish you'd never been born.

But what could you do without them
When you run out of milk and tea?
And you're daft enough to lock yourself out,
Lucky, they've got a key.

There's an Aussie, who has just moved in,
To the house across the way.
He couldn't have heard of our rain and fogs,
For all he can say is – 'Goo'day!'

What a funny bunch, us Limeys are,
We can choose to disagree.
But, it takes a lot, to admit our faults,
On that you can agree.

A VISIT TO THE HOSPITAL

Is this the way to the Pharmacy?
An attendant halts, he looks at me.
"Crikey mate! Why can't you see?"
"It's straight down there, for the Pharmacy."

Glancing up, I see a sign,
Follow the arrows, to section nine.
So far, so good – I'm doing fine,
I'll soon be there, at the Pharmacy.

A bloke pushing a trolley passes me by,
He gives me a wink, I heave a sigh.
Can anyone tell me, I wonder why,
It's so hard to find the Pharmacy!

This way, that way, round and about,
I ask a Nurse, but she knows nowt!
I darned well feel like starting to shout,
"For Pete's sake – where's the Pharmacy?"

When told, it's been reorganised,
Being here so long, I'm traumatised.
I'll need to be hospitalised,
And tell 'em "Go stuff their Pharmacy!"

My legs are aching, I need a rest,
I started out feeling full of zest.
Now I am so fed up, and *really* depressed,
I'm going home! – Gonna find a Chemists!

SIMPLY THE BEST
(DEDICATED TO MY FRIEND)

Mary, Mary- plain as any name can be,
But the one I know,
Is surely not so,
She is more than a friend, is Mary.

Full of fun, and the good she's done,
Would fill a book!
And when I chance to look,
I'll see her smile,
Which stands out a mile,
What could I do without Mary?

So whenever I'm blue, know not what to do.
I think of a lass called Mary,
She brightens my day,
And no longer I say,
I am sad, - for that's bad,
She won't have it, not she, - Not Mary!

MY OLD GAMP!

Its long life was over,
No good any more.
There it stands useless,
Against the hall door.

Near glossy new umbrellas,
Feeling sad and forlorn.
Its spokes bent and rusty,
Handle crooked and worn.

Its glory days ended,
When conceited and new.
Held up high and haughty,
For all the world to view.

When it was young,
And well in its prime.
It poked someone's eyes out,
Many a time!

But that musty old gamp,
Has stopped any fear.
Of being soaked to the skin,
And saved many a tear.

So remember the day,
This battered umbrella,
Was once used and loved,
By a jolly fine fella.

Me!

IT ALL WENT UP THE SPOUT!

Help! I need a favour –
Please get me out of this mess!
Everything I do, seems to go awry,
I'm hopeless – I confess.

My home could be a mansion,
But I haven't got the knack,
Nothing seems to go right for me,
It's more a bloomin' shack!

I advertised for a handy man,
Though he seemed a nice enough bloke,
He almost set the house alight,
It nearly went up in smoke!

He'd fixed me a plug extension,
Now I really don't like to scoff,
As I switch the light on in the hall,
The one in the kitchen goes off!

And then the gutter was leaking,
I thought – he'll sort it out!
But when he tried to have a go,
It all went up the spout!

For when we have a downpour,
Storms and gales, or squalls,
The rain gushes down my windowpanes,
It looks like Niagara Falls!

He built a fence, six foot high,
It looked good without a doubt,
The reason for this work of art,
Was to keep the animals out.

For under my window they scream and fight,
While I'm asleep in my bed,
Though the fence was meant to keep them out,
They jump over the wall instead!

A new lock I had put on my door,
He brought a reversible socket,
Now to lock the door, I open it,
And to open the door, I lock it!

Nothing seems to go right for me,
My video's gone up the spout,
The telly – it blew up on me,
I'm cursed without a doubt!

We own a musical chiming clock,
It stands on the Mantelpiece,
But at six o'clock, it booms out ten!
Wonders will never cease!

Now if you can't beat 'em, join 'em!
I'd thought I could be the same,
So I keep my bread in the biscuit tin,
And I've only myself to blame.

My flour you'll find in the coffeepot,
And tea in the flour bin,
The coffee is where the tea should be,
It shows the state I'm in!

Deciding then I'd had enough,
I asked – 'Now look here Jack,
How can you say you're a handy man?'
'Why?' he says – 'I only live over the back!

DRAKE'S GLUM!?

The boy stood on the burning deck,
His tears ran thick and fast!
The flames were fierce and licking
Right up the bloomin' mast.

This boy who stood on the burning deck,
His hands upon his hips.
All he could see now, from his post,
Was a mile of blazing ships!

Turning to the mate he said –
"Now where the hell is Drake?"
"Oh! he's up on the Hoe, playing with his bowls,
He really takes the cake!"

Then, - "Sorry I'm late," – was Drake's face red!
"How did you all get on?"
He asked one of the few, left of the crew,
"Can't tell you – they've all gone!"

Drake, now shaken and surprised,
When of the rout he learns.
The moral of this tale is such,
'You can't fiddle while Rome burns!'

UNFINISHED SYMPHONY

My Symphony of life ripened,
when one magical ray
of sunshine brought me my love,
forever more, to stay.

Life full of promise, with
music, love and play.
Now a sky of cloud surrounds me,
for my love was taken away.

The music plays on and
I wait for the day,
When my Symphony of life is finished,
and skies, no longer grey.

BOO HOO!

Oh! What a to do,
I had the flu.
Now he's got it too,
Who? My Brother Hugh.
He lives in Crewe,
With his girlfriend Sue.
She's a bit of a Shrew,
And this is quite true.

It's a real hulla-balloo,
He has got into.
Who? My Brother Hugh.
I know what I'd do,
I would bid her Adieu!
I met *my* Waterloo.
When in Katmandu,
Or was it Kew?

But that was taboo,
More than I could chew.
So with no more ado,
As this bosh is untrue,
I'm off to Peru.
Toodle-oo!

ISOLATION, - I AM DEAF!

In my quiet world, I hear no sound,
Of children playing all around.
Bells ring, birds sing, but I found,
All are lost, in my quiet world.

Troublous noise, I care not to hear,
Clamour of traffic, on motorway near.
The crash of thunder, a cry of fear,
None can intrude my quiet world.

When it became, to me quite clear,
With a little effort, in my wish to hear.
I overcame, with an aid for my ear,
Now I can choose, when to leave, my quiet world.

Had common sense, not conquered pride,
My wish to hear in my eventide,
The sounds I loved – and be denied,
A welcome reprieve, from my quiet world.

Yet my life, how would it be?
If I were blind and could not see,
All the beauty surrounding me,
I thank God, in my quiet world –

For my sight.

DUSK

The long hard day is over, soft night is nigh,
Close enveloping folds of dusk gently fall,
Clasping tight, all in its sheltering arms,
Caressing, defying what ever may befall.

Flickering lights, begin to twinkle and shine,
As one by one, they flower and grow,
Piercing the darkened world beneath,
As if to match the firefly and glow.

A mellow waning moon peeps, from behind
its shelter, from the thickening cloud,
That masses across a defenceless sky,
Covering all with a threatening shroud.

It is time now to prepare for sleep,
Mother Nature holds all in her warm embrace,
Till another dawn begins and a welcoming Sun,
Climbs high in the sky, bestowing its grace.

The skylark awakes, and begins its song.
Throwing his heart up into the sky,
A new day has begun and all is well,
Till dusk falls once more, and the Moon hangs high.

UP THE POLE (A TALL STORY!)

Don't ask them how it happened,
They didn't know themselves.
Suddenly, we had no water.
We couldn't wash ourselves.

What was worse, we couldn't make,
A welcome cup of tea.
With not a drop of water,
I ask you! How could we?

Installing a phone extension,
We needed another pole.
Along came a couple of wonders,
To dig a second hole.

You can guess now, what had happened,
The drill it pierced the main!
And the plans they had to start with,
Were all washed down the drain!

There was water, water everywhere,
But not a drop to drink!
Ah! Now here comes the gaffer,
Kicking up a stink!

He calls them a bunch of cowboys,
They'd really cooked their goose.
It was getting late and dark by now,
To continue was no use!

A plumber he is sent for,
He gives a nervous cough.
Wrenches with force a stubborn tap,
And breaks the damned thing off!

Daylight came, and so did a crane,
On the back of a dirty great lorry.
As it came into view, we saw on it too,
A telegraph pole – 'How Jolly!'

The crane it lifts, the pole in the air,
Ready to set in the ground.
As the pole starts to sway that way and this,
My heart begins to pound.

For this was outside my window,
And only yards away.
What was the betting, they'd drop the lot,
It comes crashing through my Bay!

I hold my breath, I shut my eyes,
Waiting for the crunch.
They've been messing about, it seems for hours,
And now I've missed me lunch!

As luck was in, Pole finds the hole,
And it is shoved inside.
It stands there now as regal as you like,
A notice stuck on its side –

'Anyone attempting to remove this pole!!
Is liable to a fine.'
Now how the blazes can they do that?
Your guess is as good as mine!

JUNK MAIL

Another heap of paperwork, lands on your mat,
You heave a big sigh – when will it stop?
Picking up this heap of unwanted junk,
Adverts and suggestions, when where to shop.

Pizza Parlours and take-a-ways,
For those preferring quick meals.
Pages and pages show cars galore,
To hopefuls – all seeking good deals.

Now this happens, week after week,
No matter how much we complain.
Don't they know, where it all ends up?
Out in the dustbin, there to remain.

MUM'S THE WORD

Florence Nightingale!
Her name it brings to mind,
A person of integrity,
One most noble and so kind.

Someone who puts others first,
Those who are most in need,
Of love, care and attention,
No matter how tough the deed.

There are many, many others,
If you care to look you'll see,
I've one of the very same calibre,
And she's all the world to me.

Who's this worthy lady I speak of?
One can seek, yet find no other,
You may ask, and I'll tell you now,
This lady, - she's my mother!

JUST DOODLING!

1. ANNA BOLIC
2. BOB SLEIGH
3. CATHERINE WHEEL
4. DEN MARK
5. EVA REDDY
6. FRANK ENSTEIN
7. GRACE FULL
8. HAZEL NUTT
9. IVOR COLD
10. JOHN QUILL
11. KITTY HAWK
12. LUCY LASTIC
13. MONA LOTT
14. NORA BONE
15. OLIVE OIL
16. PERCY VERE
17. QUEENIE SHEBA
18. RHODA DENDRON
19. SAL VOLATILE
20. TOM A. HAWK
21. ULY SEES
22. VIOLET RAY
23. WALTER FALL
24. X. E. CUTIONER
25. YUGO SLAVIA
26. ZAC. R. IUS

MY VENICE

Set like a jewel in a Silvery Sea,
There's no other place, I'd choose to be.
Inspired by Poets and Artists, who acclaim,
Its beauty, from all quarters they came.

St Mark's its wonders, steeped in time,
A Regal Campanile, - its bell like chime.
The Doge's Palace, stately and renowned,
Viewing it with awe, its beauty can astound.

By the lapping waters of the Grand Canal there,
Lulled by gently rocking of Gondolas where,
You will find hidden recesses of this Enchanted Isle,
Whose ghostly figures do inspire yet beguile.

Never tiring of tracing its terrain,
You'll want to return, again yet again.
To explore this Jewel in a silver sea.
Venice, - Its Magic is there, for you and for me.

JOBS

What jobs have I to do today?
That's a good question indeed, I say.
From dawn to dusk, all is sweat and grind,
It's get ready, get set, let's go you find.

What's the weather like? is first you ask,
And begin to plot your No. 1 task.
The larder's empty, now that's a must,
After you've swept and settled the dust.

Where's me trolley then, me bag and me money?
Strewth! Shopping for a family isn't all honey!
You get to the shops, what's top of the list?
Spotting plenty of offers, you just can't resist.

Mountains of goodies and bargains galore,
"Buy one, get one free," is hard to ignore.
Oh! It's started to rain, you must hurry back,
There's all this shopping, you have to unpack.

As you open your door, you heave a sigh,
It's – "What's for dinner Mum?" the usual cry.
Good – it's all quiet now, the time I like best,
I'll put me feet up, and have a rest.

Times up – you've had your whack,
"I'll do some ironing, before they come back!"
Meaning the kids, but bless 'em all,
The long, the short and the tall.

We wouldn't be without them, that we agree,
Now here comes the gaffer, wanting his tea.
The days nearly over, it's twilight once more,
But what has tomorrow for us in store?

Another hundred and one jobs, that's for sure.
Doesn't it go to show though! That's what Mums are for.

IMAGES

What images does the Summer evoke,
As you sit idling the hours away,
Remembering with a hint of a smile,
You forget it's now a cold winter's day.

How the sound of a mower disturbed your nap,
And that madman on a motorbike, zooming by.
He wound up in a heap, the silly clot,
After a few mishaps and wondered why.

The sound of a Thrush, throwing out his song,
Way up on the bough of a Sycamore tree,
Children's voices on the Summer breeze,
Scents of flowers, a humming bee.

Then the Ice Cream Van belching out loud,
"Boys and Girls come out to play,"
Lining up hopefully with hands outstretched,
For, "A Cornet Mister!" You'd hear them say.

And high up there in a cloudless sky,
The silver flash of an Aeroplane,
On its way to heaven knows where,
Perhaps to Arcadia and back again!

MISTY MEMORIES

As I sit alone with my music,
On this quiet afternoon,
My thoughts they stray to days long gone,
Hours of bliss ending, sadly too soon.

When time it had no meaning,
For my lover and I,
Truly blessed, we were as one,
The memory brings tears to my eye.

For music it was
That brought us together,
Thinking such happiness
Could go on and last forever.

Alas! Now music has no meaning,
Though forever lingers on,
Now only his memory and his music
Stay, but my lover, - he is gone.

DID IT REALLY HAPPEN?

'Twas 'The Battle of Trafalgar,'
The guns were blazing fast.
Each man doing his duty,
As it if were his last.

Cannons firing, men lay dying,
Things were looking grim.
Those Frenchies fought back bravely,
It was either sink or swim.

Nelson – Afraid? No – he would fight,
Steadfast to country and king.
He put his telescope to his eye,
But he couldn't see a thing!

The air now filled with acrid smoke,
Crew tired, spent and tardy.
Horatio firmly stands his ground,
There at his side, mate Hardy.

Suddenly Nelson gives a shout,
'I've been shot! – I'm feeling rough.'
'Kiss me Hardy!' but the answer's 'Not now,'
'I'm off – I've had enough!'

'TWAS ONE OF THOSE DAYS!

The wind is blowing, the snow is snowing,
And I can't peg out me smalls!
Oh! What a bore, when I open the door,
And the snow's piled high 'gainst the walls.

If it's not snow, we get buckets of rain,
We finish up nigh on Aquatic.
"Oh! To be in England, now April's here!"
Tho' I really must be Phlegmatic.

Try and keep cool and then you will find,
Though things aren't going your way.
Hang on for a bit and then you'll see,
Tomorrow *is* a lovely day.

A PAIR OF PANTS

When is a pair of pants,
Not a pair of pants?
If another was there,
Then it would be a pair.
It's a ruddy racket,
Only one in a packet.
How can it be a pair?
When one is not there.
All very distressing,
When one is missing.
Now it's just not fair,
For there wasn't a pair.
Oh! I know now Jack!
I'll buy another pack.

Bingo! Now I've got a pair!

THE CRUISE

You've now scoured all the brochures,
Until you're blue in the face,
Gone and checked your Bank account,
And now you've chosen the place.

In spite of all the wet blankets,
You go ahead with your scheme.
A Cruise! It sounds just dandy!
But then – "Are you chasing a dream?"

Now this is just what you'd hoped for,
Long ago when just a lass.
It was likened to the end of the world,
Never likely to come to pass.

But those doubting days are over,
Opportunity has come your way.
Lady luck has pointed a finger,
Now you've only to name the day.

That day has come, you're set to go,
You can't contain your zest.
You've packed, tickets, passport – you're ready,
What's missing? Oh! Go blow the rest.

A smashing day, fine sunny and warm,
It really couldn't be better.
Made a mental note of all your needs,
Right down to the last bloomin' letter.

The Taxi's late, "That's a fine start!"
We've got to get to the Dock.
All set! We're out on the road now,
But keeping one eye on the clock.

There she is! What a splendid sight,
Decked out with flags and bunting.
Your holiday home, for the next 10 days,
Isn't it just too exciting!

Gibraltar, Malta, Corfu and back,
To Madeira, Majorca then Spain.
Sighting Sandy beaches, mountains high,
Sunsets never to see again.

Getting to know people, speaking foreign tongues,
Chatting and making new friends.
What a pleasure cruise this has been!
But all good things they say, have to end.

With a last night farewell gala,
We all dress up, fit to kill.
Dining and dancing, till early dawn,
"Goodbye" See you again? – "You bet, your life we will!"

HARVEST TIME

Eagerly the Skylark flaps its wings,
As he flies up, up in cloudless sky.
Below the countryside, a golden glow,
For it is harvest time, and the corn is high.

Labouring reapers, spaced among the ricks,
A pitiless sun burns and the air is stilled.
Ne'er a breath of wind, to cool a brow,
No time to waste, till each wain is filled.

Not a soul rests, till the sun has set,
For there's rain in the offing, black clouds await.
They must toil and sweat, till every sheaf,
Have all been bundled, and set up straight.

Then will be time to mop a brow,
And heave a sigh of blessed relief,
Sup a cup, refreshed, can breathe again,
For how they toiled, is beyond belief.

The sun has set, all must depart,
To Harvest home and time to dream.
Another year has flown, and again once more,
The skylark wings high, o'er lush fields of green.

OUR STREET

They'll always be a Welcome,
For you, when down our street.
As the kind of folks who live here,
Are the best you'd wish to meet.

Whatch'er me ol' cock sparrers!
This greeting, you'll be bound,
To hear on all street corners,
Bet yer a penny, to a pound.

For there's none can beat a Cockney,
Even cheerful when he's down.
You'll discover his kind of humour,
From here to Canning Town.

It you chance to be around our way,
Ask anyone you meet,
Where to find humanity and warmth,
Yeah! Here, right down our street!

'HOW'S ZAT!'

An aerial view over Trent Bridge,
Picks out a cricket match, in full swing.
Those boys from down under, are battling away,
Defiant, determined their minds on one thing.

To beat their opponents, by hook or by crook,
And take home the Trophy, there on display.
Runs are clocked up, the tension grows,
Until clouds gather, and rain stops play.

Yet this does not dampen the jubilant horde,
Who continue to clamour and shout, so that
As each ball is delivered they bellow and cheer,
Even louder at the bowlers – 'How's Zat!'

Tho' the Umpire stands firm, looks unperturbed,
Ignoring the jeers and whistles, unbowed,
The match continues, more runs are scored,
And unceasing, the rumpus from the noisy crowd.

But if I were one of those spectators there,
And had to endure that uproar all day.
I'd stuff those whistles right where they belong,
And make for the gate and a clean get-away!

MISGIVINGS

If only I could write a book,
No matter, for how long it took.
My hero he'd be a dashing knave,
His wish our heroine to enslave.

He'd charm her, with his fancy speech,
To the highest heavens, with her he'd reach.
Carry her off to far away lands,
Of luminous skies, and sun drenched sands.

Beguile her with his praise galore,
(Tho' he had his eye on the girl next door!)
But our hero – he'd be not so slick,
Our heroine now, no giddy chick.

Would see right through his loquacious patter,
And think of ways his myth to shatter.
Arrange and plan, a tête à tête,
To pledge their troth, and celebrate.

Then our hero, in for a big surprise,
Would find he couldn't believe his eyes!
Have no idea of our heroine's plan,
Until, - "How D'ya like to meet my old Man?"

KIDS STUFF

A long time ago, when just a kid,
No limit to the things we did.
Running barefoot down to the moat,
Picnics – buttys, cakes we'd tote.
A lemonade bottle, now full of tea,
Hopping and skipping, and jumping with glee.

Summers were long then, the sun ever shone,
We were happy, as the day was long.
A jam jar we'd take, with handles of string,
To put our tiddlers and tadpoles in.
Caught with a net, trying not to pitch,
Into a green and slime filled ditch.

We knew our Mum would be annoyed,
If she found out, but we enjoyed
Our fun and frolics, no time to mope,
As over a tree branch, we'd throw a rope.
And back and forth, in the air we'd swing,
As carefree as the birds in Spring.

Picking buttercups in a meadow near,
And into a blackbird's nest we'd peer.
Scrumping apples in an orchard, where,
A sign saying – 'No trespassing so – beware'.
Did not deter us from having our fun,
As all kids do, till the setting sun.

'Stop getting under my feet' – Mum would say,
'Get your coats on, - go out and play.'
Not needing much prompting, we're off like a shot,
With a warning from Mum, which we soon forgot.
'Don't go too far – Tea's ready at five,'
'And be home before Father, or he'll skin you alive.'

So over the sandhills – along the lanes,
Down to the station, to watch the trains.
Leaned over a fence, near a stile,
There'll be an engine along in a while.
And then in the distance, we'd see smoke,
Pouring from firebox, well stocked with coke.

Never tiring of this splendid sight,
We'd wave and whistle, in sheer delight.
Now feeling hungry, we'd turn, and go back,
Over the bridge, that crossed the track.
We must hurry – they'll wonder where,
We've all got to – and Dad! He'll go spare!

'That's enough – d'you hear what I said?
In here you lot, now get up to bed.'
What have I told you, I'll teach you to fight!'
There was no supper – for us that night!
We knew we gave Mum a real pain in the neck,
It's a wonder, she wasn't a nervous wreck!

Dad crafty, he'd keep out of her way,
And be off to his local, if he had his pay.
Now things weren't then all milk and honey,
No one possessed a mint of money.
Yet we were rich in so many ways,
And I'd give much, for those far off days.

Oh! – What we had then, none can repeat,
Memories of times some sad, some sweet.
Some times we laughed – sometimes we cried,
Sometimes – if only – we dreamed, we sighed.
Legacies of child-hood, are flown all too fast,
So make the most of them – while they last.

HAIL, GLORIOUS SPRING!

Welcome to Spring, the Winter has flown,
The warmth of the Sun, I feel on my face.
Suddenly the pulse leaps at the thought of it,
So glad am I, my heart starts to race.

Gone are the gloomy days of Winter,
When all around was sombre and still.
With the promise of Summer days ahead,
I cannot wait to get my fill.

No longer the trees are naked and sere,
As they burst forth in new shades of green.
Matching the brightness of daffodils there,
Like clusters of burnished gold they gleam.

Soon the Butterfly on gossamer wing,
Flutters happily onto haughty rose.
Amid myriads of countless blossom where,
Every beauteous flower grows.

As if in thanks for the new born Spring,
The Thrush, he throws his song to the Sky.
Heralding the birth of long Summer days, and
The heart bursts with joy, for you and I.

AN ODE TO MOTHER'S DAY

On Mother's day you have time to think,
How the years fly by before you can blink!
One moment your bairns are cute and small,
Then before you know it, they're five feet tall!

With them you've gone through sickness and health,
And not for you were dreams of wealth!
For the greatest wealth for me is this,
Being your Mother is one I would not miss!

Brushing aside any urge to weep,
I count my blessings each night I sleep!
So remember children, I can only say,
A big 'Thank you too, on Your Mother's Day!'

GUY FAWKES NIGHT

Guy, - poor bloke, will never know,
Or even guessed what he had in store,
As crash! Bang! Wallop! Whoosh! and 'Whizz!
Another Rocket with an Almighty roar
Ploughs its way up, up into a sky,
Filled already with Fireworks galore.

This pastime's been going on for years,
Ever since someone foiled Fawkes' plot,
And poor Guy found he was a laughing stock,
For his copybook, he did blot.

Now once a year the kids have fun,
As perched on a bonfire, Guy poor bloke,
Goes up in flames, - a sight to see,
This would be Knave, now goes up in smoke

The moral of this, - do not play with fire!

CHRISTMAS PRESENCE

Oh! What a lovely time it be
With twinkling lights on a Christmas tree,
Decked out with Holly and Mistletoe,
The ground outside all covered in snow.

Queues in the High Streets everywhere,
Shopping for gifts and things to wear,
Buses filled with shoppers willing to spend
The housekeeping money, you *can* depend!

"Forget about it" they probably say,
And carry on preparing for Christmas Day,
That day arrives and so it begins,
Welcoming Aunt Olive, with her double chins.

Gran's wheeled in, in her mobile chair,
Swearing this is the last time, she'll be there,
While Dad's outside sweeping up snow,
Mum's stuck at the gas stove, having a go.

Stuffing the Turkey, her face flushed and red,
"Stone the crows" she says, - "Wish I'd stayed in bed!"
Aunt Fanny now, seems bright and merry,
Looks as if she's been at the sherry.

Dad comes in, wiping his boots,
Shouts at the kids, - they don't care two hoots,
They can't wait, for the time to come,
To open their presents, Tommy wants a gun.

Little brother Jim, now he'd like a bike,
"You'll be lucky" says Mum, "Santa's gone on strike."
Now Jim's not stupid, he knows it's his Mum,
"You can't fool me," he says, "I'm not that dumb."

Now dinner's over, the Turkey was good,
Dad lays back in his chair, full of Plum Pud,
They all take their places by the tree,
As Santa arrives, amid whoops of glee.

All the presents are opened, one by one,
Young Jim's got his bike, Tommy his gun,
And Aunt Olive's in her element,
With a top up of her 'Yardley' Scent.

There are Oohs! and Ahs! all over the place,
Complete with smiles on everyone's face,
Dad's chuffed, a case of his favourite beer!
Mum's got the new pinny, - she gets every year!

The feasting over, the guests prepare
To leave as Mum, sinks back in a chair,
"Thank Gawd, that's over for another year,"
As Dad breaks open a can of beer.

There's no denying Christmas is fun,
But a lot of hard work, for poor old Mum,
She can now put her feet up, and have no fear,
She won't be budging till "Happy New Year!"

HATCHED, MATCHED AND DESPATCHED

"Cor stone the Crows!" Mum was saying
As she entered the room, shaking her head.
"Just as I feared, there's another on the way,
And I felt sure it was all that new bread!"

Poor Dad looked up in amazement,
Nodding agreement at his trouble and strife.
For this was the last thing they'd planned for,
In the unruffled Autumn of life.

Dawned the day, her time had come,
Mum bore Eddie, a fine healthy boy.
She was more than highly delighted,
As she gazed at her bundle of joy.

Years flew by, little Eddie grew up,
He joined the local Brass Band.
Catching the eye of the village flirt,
Things quickly got out of hand.

For blowing his trumpet, in more ways than one,
Our Eddie was taken for a ride.
Before he knew it, he was up that Aisle,
On his arm, a satisfied Bride.

For she had played her cards right enough,
Taking Eddie for all he could give.
When things they went from bad to worse,
He lost the will to live.

Not knowing now which way to turn,
Having used up all his resources,
In pandering to her every whim,
Ed left home and joined the Forces!

Leaving behind a 'Soldiers Farewell,'
Boarded ship with his Platoon.
Bound for a port unknown to him,
Lands up in farthest Rangoon.

There making hay while the sun shines,
He'll no longer need out pity.
For the last we heard of poor old Ed,
He was sitting mighty pretty!

Laying back in the arms of a dusky maid,
Being fanned by a 'Punkah Wallah',
"Would we change places with our lucky Ed?
You can bet your bottom dollar!"

THOSE DAYS WHEN

In the evening of life, you can recall,
The innocence and wonder you had when small,
Safe in the haven of your Mother's grasp,
As you tight against her breast she'd clasp.

The look of love upon her face,
A smile benign, none can replace,
Your tiny fingers wound round her hands,
Creating a feeling only Mum understands.

Your first faltering steps, hesitantly tried,
Surely it showed, her feeling of pride,
And pleasure too of everyone present,
At this painstaking, yet major event.

But Baby days they flee at last,
As time and tide flies by so fast,
Then the nail biting days of schooling began,
Shaping and moulding, you into man.

You may have found the journey ahead,
Bogged down, with maybe fear and dread,
But there's ever a light, at the end of the road,
Giving you peace and hope to lighten your load.

DUNKIRK'S LITTLE SHIPS (REMEMBER?)

From humble barge, to fishing smack,
Under threat from hellish air attack.
Those little ships, prepare to sail,
To say them nay! Of no avail!

Sailing away, to peril untold,
God fearing men – steadfast and bold.
Convoys of heroes, bound for Dunkirk,
T'was not their policy, their duty to shirk.

Though little ships, but giant of heart,
No scruples, no qualms, feared not to depart.
To a hell on earth on blasted beach,
Mud covered shell-shocked troops to reach.

With dignity and pride, they patiently wait,
Prepared and ready, to accept their fate.
But for those ships, desiring no glory,
Would Dunkirk's scenario, be a different story?

These little ships return once more,
To a now naked and ghostly shore,
Lugger, Steamer and Lifeboat small,
Clipper, Ketch and Schooner tall.

We must ne'er forget these gallant men,
Who came from village, dale and glen.
Their nightmare suffering, tears and sorrow,
For our today, they dared their tomorrow!

WHAT'S A DOODLEBUG MUM?

Clouds they were lifting, the war almost won,
But was it too much to hope?
Discovering to our bitter cost,
We were on a slippery slope.

In the month of June in '44
We faced a deadlier threat.
To violate a war weary land.
Our nightmare – not over yet.

From lucid sky, a fearful drone,
It was like no sound I'd known.
Striking fear in the hearts of men,
Spellbound – I stood, as stone.

For to my eye, a fiery cross,
Discharging Hellish flame.
It ploughed a path, with insolence,
Its duty, to kill or maim.

A sinister unmanned terror,
It fell with awesome hush.
But no cowardly act, such as this,
Could our dogged spirits crush.

Innocents perished as they slept,
Or on their way to work.
Yet no tyrant, whoever they be,
Could cause our duty to shirk.

Let them despatch their pilotless plane,
Doodlebug rocket or bomb,
Had they not heard of our bulldog breed,
Who survived this maelstrom?

BLOOD RED POPPIES AT THE CENOTAPH

A sombre hush lies over the land,
Leaves float lifeless, to the ground.
Tragic memories of suffering and pain,
No excuse, no licence, to be found.
For lives wasted, freely given away,
For your tomorrow, for our today.

A signal heralds, the stroke of time,
As heads bow low, and tears flow fast,
Remember the sick, the maimed, the fallen,
Who fought the good fight, to the very last.
The valiants return, to march, heads high,
As a lonely Spitfire, sweeps through the sky.

Tributes are laid, to the many who,
Cleansed our world, from terrible threat,
Of subjection to forces, corrupt and foul,
Forever mankind, shall be in their debt.
As millions remember, the old and the young,
Lift up your voices, their praises be sung.

NOTHING IS FOREVER

When I was young,
And full of zest,
I'd take me chances
And blow the rest.

I'd scale every mountain,
And ford every stream,
Never had the time to,
Just sit and dream.

Thinking that life,
Would go on forever,
Not stopping to think,
Was not very clever.

Old Father Time,
He knew a thing or two,
It's no good biting off,
More than you can chew.

And now that I'm old,
Tho' wrinkled and grey,
Looking back at the years,
I stop and I say –

Time waits for no man,
So take it by the throat,
Grab your chances, while you can,
Or you may miss the boat!

GET CRACKING!

The Sweetest singing of the lark,
Sunbeams streaming 'cross my bed,
'Tis no time to laze around,
Arise! Get cracking, you sleepy head.

There are umpteen untold things to do,
Places to attend,
Those you always dreamed about,
So jump to it, my friend.

With a great big world out there, pal,
Don't wait, no time to lose,
It's brimming with excitement,
Love, laughter, whatever you choose.

Time it's said, waits for no man,
No faltering, you and I,
Grab and hold each moment,
Or life, - will pass you by.

MY HOME

You'd hardly call it a Mansion,
Not even classed a shack,
It's a place that's really lived in,
With ease other houses lack.

Where you can put your feet up,
Throw off daily cares and woe,
Can cock a snook at moaners,
And tell them where to go.

A garden you can rest in,
Blotting out all need to frown,
Giving you peace and comfort,
When things, they get you down.

Feeling solace and contentment,
As you gaze up at the sky,
You can put aside your worries,
And breathe a blessed sigh.

NEW HORIZONS

Living in this world of ours,
With all its faults and fears,
Through hardships, war and famine,
Suffering heartache, pain and tears.

Every day will bring its sorrows,
To each and everyone,
Sadly worse for many, and
Down to Hell for some.

But life was never meant to be
Flowing with milk and honey,
So brace yourselves for such and try
To look for Horizons, - Sunny.

Purple sunsets, - a waning moon,
Dawns arrival in full glory,
So start the day with expectancy,
And beginning, - a new story.

DAVID

There's a man in my life,
You could call him a gent,
On hand, whenever I'm in need,
In fact he is Heaven sent.

He has been with me a long time,
Ever since when just a sprout,
Through times of toil and trouble,
Good mates, - day in, day out.

We have a barney sometimes,
and don't see eye to eye,
Still, we manage to get over it,
Never met a nicer guy!

When things look bleak around you,
And you're really got the humps,
"Cuppa tea Mum?" he will call,
Plucking you out of the dumps.

What would I do without him,
Life wouldn't be the same,
Who is this Gent I talk of?
It's my son David – that is his name.

A LETTER TO MY SON

I have a picture of you sitting there,
Just pondering with furrowed brow,
Your mind ticking over, you breathe a sigh,
As the phone it rings – "What's she want now?"

But what would I do without you,
You and your expertise,
To find another, efficient as you,
As always, you aim to please.

You've pleased me no end, so thank you dear,
For everything you have done,
You've given me joy, since you were a boy,
I'm proud to call you my son.

And when you're many miles from me,
It's as if you're really here,
'Cos I can get you on the phone,
And your voice – it's always clear!

Until the day you come home to me,
My Son, I'll pray for you,
And now I'll say a fond farewell,
Cos' I'm off to bed – Toodleoo!

BARBIE GIRL

Sparkling eyes shining, happy and free,
Running and jumping, skipping with glee,
Along the lanes and through the trees,
Her long flaxen hair fanned by the breeze.

A certain melody, a plaintive tune,
Stirs up a memory, as you turn the page
Of pictures stored in the recess of mind,
Happier times in that long ago age.

Time Alas! Does never stand still
Enough to recapture those halcyon days,
When your girlie was small and very sweet,
Who grew into a lady with exceptional ways.

Not for her to shirk or go back on her word
Determined, resolute and cussed if you like,
If there's a job to be done, thorough it will be,
She's the gaffer and would tell you, - "Get on your bike."
Could we do without Barbie? – "Not on your Nelly!"

A LETTER TO MY DAUGHTER

I look out of my window,
And say to myself – Oh! Hell!
Here she comes, walking up me path,
And starts to ring my bell.

It's that blessed girl of mine,
Wants a cuppa, and a natter,
Then it's "You heard this," and "You heard that?"
But to me it doesn't matter.

I look forward, to this hour each day,
When she finds the time to pop in,
But then she gets an earful from me,
"I want you to do some shoppin!"

When on the phone I'm crafty,
With a tongue as smooth as silk,
Oh daughter dear, are you coming up?
Could you bring me a Pint of milk?

What would I do without her?
I really couldn't think,
But if one day she didn't come,
I'd narf kick up a stink!

Tho' now you know, all this is tripe,
I'm trying to be explicit,
But I want to say, now Daughter dear,
Really, I didn't mean it!

Thank you for all you do for me,
For the lovely cards and flowers,
I can sit each day and look at them,
For Hours and Hours, and Hours.